create your own calm

A JOURNAL *for* QUIETING ANXIETY

Meera Lee Patel

A TARCHERPERIGEE BOOK

To you,
for creating your own calm

tarcherperigee

An imprint of Penguin Random House LLC
penguinrandomhouse.com

This edition has been adapted from the original edition for Five Below.

ISBN: 9780593084144
Proprietary ISBN: 9781101949726

Printed in the United States of America
3 5 7 9 10 8 6 4 2

Book design by Meera Lee Patel

INTRODUCTION

This book is a journal for quieting anxiety. It is also a journal for self-acceptance. It helps you discover the peace that exists only when you feel content with who you are. It encourages you to look inside yourself to identify the roots behind your deepest (and often, most subtle) fears. It helps you dismantle your anxiety by offering techniques that quell the pangs of worry that stem from each fear. I share the practical methods for managing anxiety that helped me transition from living in fear to living in calm curiosity.

Have patience with yourself as you move through these pages at your own pace. Please remember that managing anxiety is a continual process: there is no one way to achieve peace of mind. Different methods work for different situations or periods in your life. The biggest gift you can give yourself is the chance to try again.

There is a light that exists in all dark places, and I hope these pages help you find it. Hold courage in your heart. The way you feel right now is temporary, and like everything else in life, it too will change. There are innumerable paths through the anxiety you feel, and this journal contains many of them. Each one will offer comfort for an anxious heart, lessons to carry with you, and challenges for you to navigate. Use what works and discard the rest.

Remember that if one road isn't a good fit, there are always several more: peace will inevitably follow you when you go your own way.

Work on releasing anxiety in your body:

1) Notice the places where your body feels tense or hardened.

2) Breathe in through your nose, and out through your mouth.

3) Repeat this exercise until the tension subsides.

BEFORE THIS EXERCISE, MY ANXIETY FELT LIKE:

AFTER THIS EXERCISE, MY ANXIETY FEELS LIKE:

List or draw three things that always
make you laugh and feel at ease.

TO LOVE ONE SELF IS THE BEGINNING OF A LIFELONG ROMANCE.

Oscar Wilde, *An Ideal Husband*

List three ways you are hard on yourself.

1.

2.

3.

How can you support yourself more?

YOU NEED to LEARN HOW to select your thoughts just the same way YOU SELECT YOUR CLOTHES every day. This is A POWER YOU CAN CULTIVATE.

ELIZABETH GILBERT
Eat Pray Love

Write down three anxious thoughts that frequently enter your mind. What positive thoughts can you replace each of these with?

1. Anxious thought:

   Positive thought:

2. Anxious thought:

   Positive thought:

3. Anxious thought:

   Positive thought:

The next time the anxious thought fills your mind, choose to listen to the positive thought instead.

you are never stronger...than when you land on the other side of despair.

ZADIE SMITH
White Teeth

What are you fearful about right now
that is making you anxious?

What is the likelihood this will actually happen?

What can you do if it does happen?

The source
of a true smile
is an awakened mind.

THICH NHAT HANH
Peace Is Every Step

What color does your stress feel like?
Paint or color it here.

What color does your calmness feel like?
Paint or color it here.

BE curious, NOT judg mental

Believing you <u>can</u> do something comes from a place of curiosity and confidence, while believing you <u>should</u> do something comes from a place of judgment. Learn to approach yourself with "can" instead of "should."

What is something you feel you should do?

Why do you feel you should do it?

Do you want to do it? (Circle one)

YES / NO

If the answer is no, what can you do instead?

I URGE YOU TO PLEASE notice, when you are happy, AND EXCLAIM OR MURMUR OR THINK AT SOME POINT, "If this isn't nice, I don't know what is."

List ten things you are grateful for.

1. _____

2. _____

3. _____

4. _____

5. _____

6. _____

7. _____

8. _____

9. _____

10. _____

We can easily forgive a child who is afraid of the dark; the real tragedy of life is when men are afraid of the light.

PLATO

What values are most important to you?
Circle all that apply.

KINDNESS   GRATITUDE

STRENGTH   HUMILITY

PERSEVERANCE   POSITIVITY

PASSION   INTELLIGENCE   HUMOR

STABILITY   WEALTH

FREEDOM   INDEPENDENCE   MOBILITY

HEALTH   WIT   CUNNING

CAPABILITY   GENEROSITY

ALTRUISM   ADMIRABILITY

DEDICATION   WORK ETHIC

I had the epiphany that laughter was light, and light was laughter, and that this was the secret of the universe.

DONNA TARTT, THE GOLDFINCH

Close your eyes and imagine your most beautiful life.

What does it look like? Draw or describe it here.

True happiness is... to enjoy the PRESENT, without anxious DEPENDENCE UPON the future.

LUCIUS ANNAEUS SENECA

What thoughts fill your mind when you feel anxious
about the future? List them here:

1.

2.

3.

Close your eyes and take five deep breaths.
What thoughts make you feel excited about the future?

1.

2.

3.

TO BELIEVE YOURSELF BRAVE IS TO BE BRAVE.

JOAN of ARC

What are five things you would do if you didn't feel afraid?

1.

2.

3.

4.

5.

Now close your eyes and believe you are brave.
YOU ARE BRAVE.

How will you move toward each of these five things?

1.

2.

3.

4.

5.

THERE MUST BE LOTS OF MAGIC IN
THE WORLD... BUT PEOPLE DON'T
KNOW WHAT IT IS LIKE OR HOW TO
MAKE IT. PERHAPS THE BEGINNING
IS JUST TO SAY NICE THINGS ARE
GOING TO HAPPEN UNTIL YOU MAKE
THEM HAPPEN.

Frances Hodgson Burnett
The Secret Garden

One of the best remedies for anxiety is being in nature.
Take a walk outside, being aware of everything around you.
Write down three things you see, feel, and hear.

1. I see:

2. I feel:

3. I hear:

WE OURSELVES FEEL THAT WHAT WE ARE DOING IS JUST A DROP IN THE OCEAN. BUT THE OCEAN WOULD BE LESS BECAUSE OF THAT MISSING DROP.

Mother Teresa

List five things that ONLY YOU offer to the world.

1.

2.

3.

4.

5.

You can't be brave unless you're afraid.

A TIME I WAS AFRAID:

HOW I MOVED PAST MY FEAR:

When you arise
in the morning
think on what a
precious privilege
it is to live —
to breathe — to
think — to enjoy —
to love! MARCUS AURELIUS

Breathe in and out, focusing on the gratitude
you feel for a new day.

What is a thought you are grateful for?

What is a feeling you are grateful to experience?

What is something you feel grateful to have?

Who is someone you are grateful for?

IT ISN'T ENOUGH
TO TALK ABOUT
peace.

ONE MUST
believe IN IT.

AND IT ISN'T ENOUGH
TO BELIEVE IN IT.

ONE MUST
work AT IT.

ELEANOR
ROOSEVELT

Name the things that make you feel grounded and secure.

A PERSON:

A PLACE:

A BOOK:

A SONG:

AN ACTIVITY:

Everything's a story.

YOU ARE A STORY.

I am a STORY.

FRANCES HODGSON BURNETT
A Little Princess

What story do you immediately tell yourself
when you begin to feel anxious?

What story can you tell yourself instead?

A JOURNEY OF A thousand miles BEGINS WITH a single step.

LAO TZU

Think of something that makes you feel anxious.

Write about how you feel here:

Close your fists tightly and feel the tension.
Open and release them slowly. Repeat this 10 times.

Write about how you feel now:

BEAUTY IS NOT
IN THE FACE; BEAUTY
is a light in the heart.

KHALIL GIBRAN

What are three things that give your life meaning?
Draw them here.

YOUR FEAR WILL ALWAYS LEAD YOU
to the magic.

<u>My Friend Fear</u>

What are two fears you'd like to work through?

FEAR #1:

Why I feel afraid:

What this fear is telling me I want most:

Instead of feeling afraid, I wish I felt:

I can begin feeling this way by:

FEAR #2:

Why I feel afraid:

What this fear is telling me I want most:

Instead of feeling afraid, I wish I felt:

I can begin feeling this way by:

YOU WILL BECOME WAY LESS CONCERNED WITH what other people think of you WHEN YOU REALIZE HOW SELDOM THEY DO.

DAVID FOSTER WALLACE
Infinite Jest

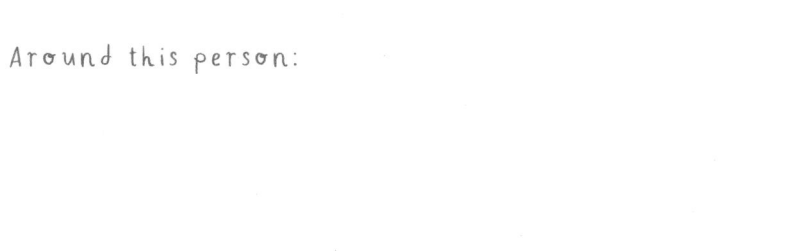

Our biggest anxieties can stem from feeling like an outsider. When do you currently feel left out?

Around this person:

In this place:

When I am:

When I think about:

When I try to do this:

The secret of life, though, is **TO FALL SEVEN TIMES** and to **GET UP EIGHT TIMES.**

PAULO COELHO
The Alchemist

Yesterday my anxiety felt like:

A DARK SHADOW   SHARP PAIN   DISCOMFORT

Today my anxiety feels like:

NEGATIVITY   PARALYSIS   DOUBT

Tomorrow, I hope my anxiety will feel:

 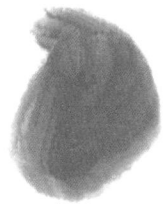 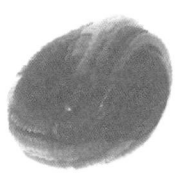

LIGHTER   QUIETER   LESS OF
AN OBSTACLE

You
are
your
best
thing.

TONI MORRISON
Beloved

Imagine yourself in your ideal future.

1. Describe how you feel in this future:

2. What are the thoughts you have?

3. How do you spend your time?

4. What is the lesson you live by?

When one door
of happiness closes,
another opens;
BUT OFTEN WE LOOK
SO LONG AT THE
CLOSED DOOR THAT WE
DO NOT SEE
the one that has
been opened for us.

HELEN KELLER
We Bereaved

List something you've lost (a job, a relationship, a loved one, a project) in the last year.

What are two positive things that came from this experience?

1.

2.

NOTHING IN LIFE IS to bE FEARED, It IS ONLY to BE UNDERSTOOD.

MARIE CURIE

What is a source of stress in each
of the following areas?

My health:

My creativity:

My family:

My friends:

At work/school:

On social media:

How can you eliminate some of these stressors?

For my health, I can:

For my creativity, I can:

With my family, I can:

With my friends, I can:

At work/school I can:

With social media, I can:

I once asked a bird,

"HOW IS IT THAT YOU FLY IN THIS GRAVITY of DARKNESS?"

She responded,

"LOVE LIFTS ME".

·HAFIZ·

What is the most recent thing someone else
did to lift your spirits?

What is the most recent thing you did
to lift someone else's spirits?

ONE
must still have
CHAOS
in oneself to be
ABLE TO GIVE BIRTH
-to a-
dANCINg
STAR.

FRIEDRICH NIETZSCHE

Write down three things that make you feel nervous.

What is an exciting possibility that also exists
inside each of these?

1. What makes me nervous:

   A possibility that exists here:

2. What makes me nervous:

   A possibility that exists here:

3. What makes me nervous:

   A possibility that exists here:

everything has
BEAUTY,

BUT NOT EVERYONE
can see.

CONFUCIUS

List something beautiful about each of the following:

YESTERDAY:

TODAY:

A TIME YOU FELT ANXIOUS:

A TIME YOU FELT JOYFUL:

LAST YEAR:

NEXT YEAR:

A NEW OPPORTUNITY:

A MISTAKE:

A RAINY DAY:

"Dear old world," SHE MURMURED, "You are very lovely and I am glad to be alive in you."

L. M. MONTGOMERY
Anne of Green Gables

What sights and sounds make you feel most calm?

List or draw them here.

IF WE WAIT UNTIL WE'RE
READY, WE'LL BE WAITING
FOR THE REST OF OUR LIVES.

LEMONY SNICKET
The Ersatz Elevator

Think of a worry you wish you could leave behind.

Close your eyes and meditate on this worry for five minutes, breathing in and out slowly and deeply.

When you open your eyes, let the worry go.

I exist AS I AM, THAT IS enough.

-WALT WHITMAN-

Instead of telling yourself you should be somewhere else, identify why where you are is enough.

FAMILY

I should feel:

Instead I feel:

What this is telling me:

WORK

I should be:

Instead I am:

What this is telling me:

SPIRIT

I should think:

Instead I think:

What this is telling me:

HEALTH

I should be:

Instead I am:

What this is telling me:

LOVE

I should feel:

Instead I feel:

What this is telling me:

All the variety, all the charm,
all the beauty of life is made
up of LIGHT and SHADOW.

LEO TOLSTOY
Anna Karenina

Choose three things you wish you could change about your life. What is the light and dark of each one?

#1:

THE LIGHT:

THE DARK:

#2:

THE LIGHT:

THE DARK:

#3

THE LIGHT:

THE DARK:

Forever is composed of nows.

EMILY DICKINSON

List five things in your life that put you at ease.

1.

2.

3.

4.

5.

LIFE
CAN ONLY BE
UNDERSTOOD
BACKWARDS;
BUT IT MUST BE
LIVED
FORWARDS.

SØREN KIERKEGAARD

What are two lessons you've learned in the past year?
How have they affected the choices
you've made since?

Lesson #1:

Choices I made because of it:

Lesson #2:

Choices I made because of it:

The more one does
and sees and feels,
the more one is
able to do.

AMELIA EARHART

Close your eyes and visualize the situation going positively.
Imagine all the details and how peaceful you feel
throughout the experience.

So many things are possible just as long as you don't know they're impossible.

NORTON JUSTER
The Phantom Tollbooth

Write down three goals that feel impossible to you.

What is one step you can take toward
making each of them possible?

1. Impossible goal:

   Possible step:

2. Impossible goal:

   Possible step:

3. Impossible goal:

   Possible step:

I AM NO BIRD;
and NO NET ENSNARES ME;
I am a free human being
WITH AN INDEPENDENT WILL.

—CHARLOTTE BRONTË—
Jane Eyre

Write a letter to your past self, identifying the ways you've grown and moved through obstacles, fears, and anxieties. Include why you are proud of yourself for choosing to keep going.

Dear Self...

The willingness to accept responsibility for one's own life is the source from which self-respect springs.

JOAN DIDION
Slouching Towards Bethlehem

CIRCLE the ways you are already taking care of your mind, body, and soul.

Then PLACE A STAR next to three things you will try to include regularly.

SETTING BOUNDARIES   CALLING A FRIEND

EATING HEALTHY FOODS   SLEEPING

CARING FOR OTHERS   EXERCISING

SOCIAL MEDIA DETOX

MEDITATING

EXPRESSING GRATITUDE

SPENDING TIME WITH LOVED ONES

DANCING   LISTENING TO MYSELF   THERAPY

TAKING TIME FOR MYSELF

SOMETHING IN ME KNOWS WHERE I AM GOING.

JACKSON POLLOCK

The Unknown can be a source of great anxiety and fear.
In these moments, it can be helpful to focus
on the things you feel confident of.

I KNOW:

I AM:

I FEEL:

I CAN:

I WANT:

IF I NEED HELP, I WILL ASK:

It will never rain roses: when we want to have roses, we must plant more roses.

GEORGE ELIOT

What are four things you want to have more of?
How can you cultivate each in your life?

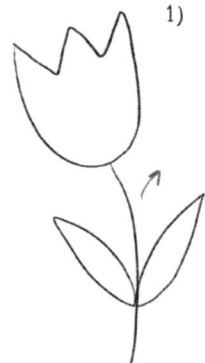

1)

2)

3)

4)

We are all strangers in a
strange land, longing for
HOME, but not quite
knowing WHAT or WHERE
home is.

MADELEINE L'ENGLE
The Rock That is Higher

When do you feel most peaceful?
Write or draw about it in this home.

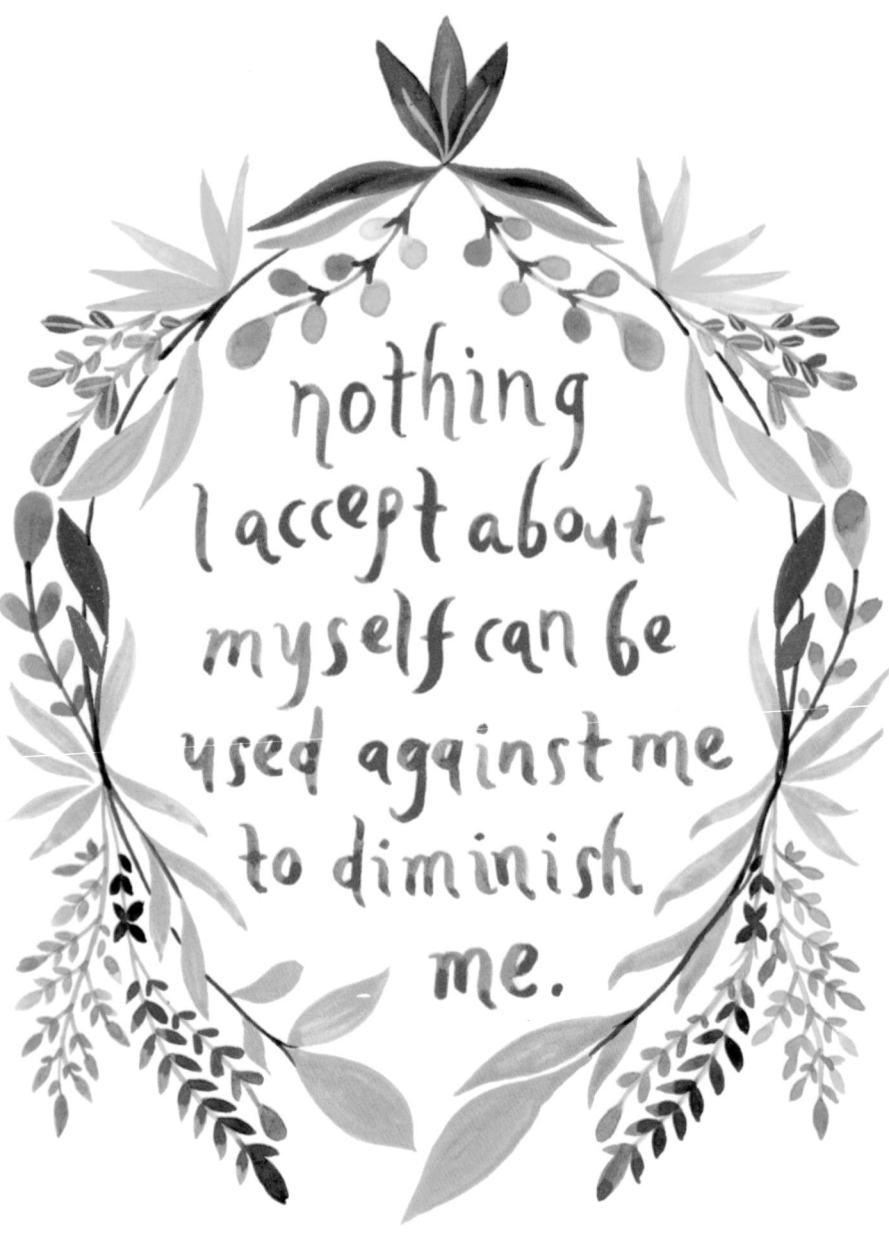

nothing
I accept about
myself can be
used against me
to diminish
me.

Audre Lorde
<u>Sister Outsider</u>

What is a trait (physical or emotional) you wish you could
change about yourself?

List three ways this can be a source of strength for you.

1.

2.

3.

Within you, there is a **stillness** and a **sanctuary** to which you can retreat at anytime and be **yourself.**

HERMANN HESSE

Siddhartha

Step outside and breathe in air, sun, and trees.

Observe what you see, smell, and hear.

Notice how your mind quiets and your body relaxes.

Remember that there is always a new day close by.

THE MOST COMMON WAY PEOPLE GIVE UP *their* POWER IS BY THINKING *they don't* HAVE ANY.

Alice Walker

Describe (or think about) a situation
you currently feel powerless in.

What is one action you can take to change the situation?

WORST POSSIBLE OUTCOME:

BEST POSSIBLE OUTCOME:

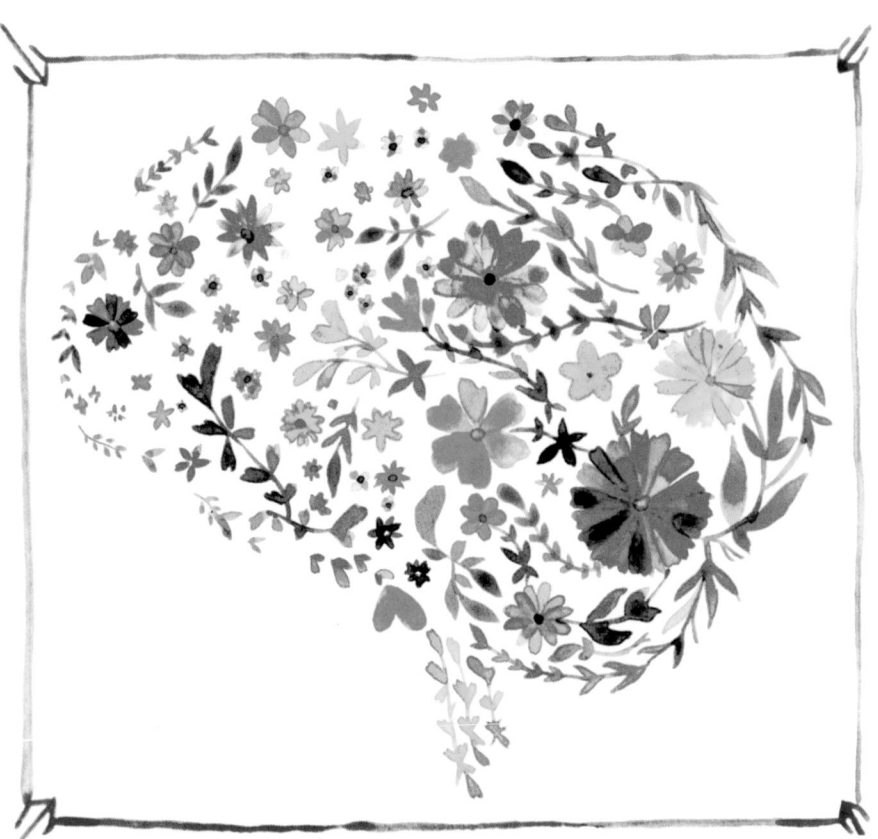

What you're supposed to do when you don't like a thing is CHANGE IT. If you can't change it, CHANGE THE WAY YOU THINK ABOUT IT.

MAYA ANGELOU
Wouldn't Take Nothing
for My Journey Now

WHAT I DON'T LIKE	HOW I CAN CHANGE IT	HOW I CAN THINK ABOUT IT

Life is like RIDING A BICYCLE TO KEEP YOUR BALANCE, YOU MUST KEEP moving.

ALBERT EINSTEIN

ACTION CHANGES ATTITUDE.

What is one action that always resets your mood?

My advice is,

NEVER DO TOMORROW WHAT YOU CAN DO TODAY.

Procrastination is the thief of time.

CHARLES DICKENS
David Copperfield

I am avoiding _____

_____ .

because I'm afraid of _____

_____

_____ .

Reframe the task as a mantra that helps you
move forward with courage:

_____ is an opportunity for me

to grow, learn, and _____

_____ .

Repeat this mantra to yourself
as often as needed as you move forward.

IF you dare NOTHING, then when the day is over, NOTHING is all you will have gained.

NEIL GAIMAN
The Graveyard Book

Write down three big dreams you are afraid of pursuing. Which fear is keeping you from pursuing each one? What action will move you past this fear?

1. BIG DREAM:

   Fear stopping me:

   Action that will move me forward:

2. BIG DREAM:

   Fear stopping me:

   Action that will move me forward:

3. BIG DREAM:

   Fear stopping me:

   Action that will move me forward:

IF ONE SCHEME OF HAPPINESS FAILS,
human nature turns to another;
IF THE FIRST CALCULATION IS WRONG,
we make a second better;
WE FIND COMFORT SOMEWHERE.

JANE AUSTEN
Mansfield Park

I PLANNED FOR THIS:

BUT INSTEAD THIS HAPPENED:

AND I GOT THROUGH IT BY:

Nothing contributes so much to tranquilize the mind as a steady purpose.

MARY SHELLEY
Frankenstein

What does a hopeful and secure future look like to you?

What are three steps you can take toward
building that future?

1.

2.

3.

Every individual matters.

Every individual has a role to play.

Every individual makes a difference.

JANE GOODALL

Fill out this Venn diagram about yourself.

WHY I MATTER

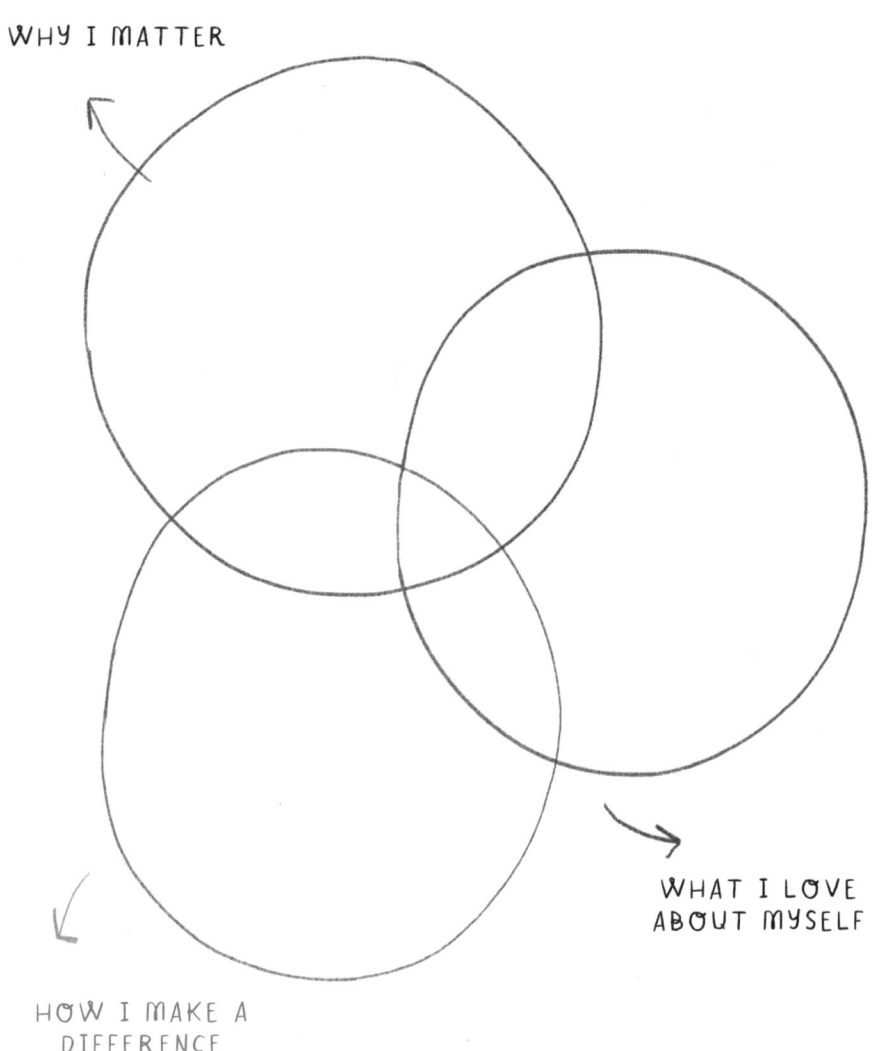

WHAT I LOVE
ABOUT MYSELF

HOW I MAKE A
DIFFERENCE

THERE ARE TWO WAYS of SPREADING
LIGHT: TO BE THE CANDLE or THE
MIRROR THAT RECEIVES IT.

EDITH WHARTON

Ways I can shine light and be supportive when...

A friend is disappointed:

I am disappointed:

A friend is feeling worried:

I am feeling worried:

A friend is scared:

I am scared:

A friend is excited:

I am excited:

A friend is sad:

I am sad:

BIBLIOGRAPHY

Quotations appear from the following publications:

Anna Karenina by Leo Tolstoy (Wordsworth Classics, 1997)

Anne of Green Gables by L. M. Montgomery (Signet, 2003)

The Alchemist by Paulo Coelho (HarperTorch, 2006)

The New Beacon Book of Quotations by Women by Rosalie Maggio (Beacon Press, 1992)

Beloved by Toni Morrison (Vintage, 2004)

The Best Liberal Quotes Ever: Why the Left is Right by William Martin (Sourcebooks, 2004)

Complete Works of George Eliot by George Eliot (Delphi Classics, 2012)

Conversations with Artists by Selden Rodman (Capricorn, 1961)

Daniel Deronda by George Eliot (Penguin Classics, 1996)

David Copperfield by Charles Dickens (Macmillan Collector's Library, 2016)

Einstein: His Life and Universe by Walter Isaacson (Simon & Schuster, 2007)

Eleanor Roosevelt, Voice of America broadcast (November 11, 1951)

The Ersatz Elevator by Lemony Snicket (HarperCollins, 2001)

The Fra: For Philistines and Roycrofters, edited by Elbert Hubbard, Felix Shay (Hubbard Journals, 1913)

Frankenstein: The 1818 Text by Mary Shelley (Penguin Classics, 2018)

The Gift: Poems by Hafiz, the Great Sufi Master by Hafiz (Penguin Books, 1999)

The Goldfinch by Donna Tartt (Back Bay Books, 2015)

The Graveyard Book by Neil Gaiman (HarperCollins, 2010)

Harry Potter and the Goblet of Fire by J. K. Rowling (Scholastic Paperbacks, 2002)

An Ideal Husband by Oscar Wilde (Project Gutenberg, 2009)

Infinite Jest by David Foster Wallace (Back Bay Books, 2006)

Jane Eyre by Charlotte Brontë (Bantam Classics, 1981)

The Journals of Søren Kierkegaard (Princeton University Press)

A Little Princess by Frances Hodgson Burnett (Puffin Books, 2014)

Mansfield Park by Jane Austen (Wordsworth Editions Ltd, 1998)

A Man Without a Country by Kurt Vonnegut (Random House Trade Paperbacks, 2007)

My Friend Fear by Meera Lee Patel (TarcherPerigee, 2018)

Our Precarious Habitat by Melvin A. Benarde (W. W. Norton & Company, 1973)

Peace Is Every Step: The Path of Mindfulness in Everyday Life by Thich Nhat Hanh (Bantam, 1992)

Personal Recollections of Joan of Arc, Volume 1 by Mark Twain (Project Guteberg, 2018)

The Annotated Phantom Tollbooth by Norton Juster (Knopf, 2011)

The Rock That Is Higher: Story as Truth by Madeleine L'Engle (Convergent, 2018)

The Secret Garden by Frances Hodgson Burnett (HarperClassics, 2010)

Siddhartha by Hermann Hesse (Samaira Book Publishers, 2018)

Sister Outsider: Essays and Speeches by Audre Lorde (Crossing Press, 2007)

Slouching Towards Bethlehem by Joan Didion (Farrar, Straus and Giroux, 2008)

Soaring Wings: A Biography of Amelia Earhart by George Palmer Putnam (1939)

Song of Myself by Walt Whitman (Dover Publications, 2000)

Stories Told by Mother Teresa by Edward Le Joly and Jaya Chaliha (Element Books, 2000)

Tao Te Ching by Lao Tzu (Harper Perennial Modern Classics, 2006)

Thus Spoke Zarathustra by Friedrich Nietzsche (Modern Library, 1995)

"Vesalius in Zante (1564)" by Edith Wharton in *North American Review* (November 1902)

We Bereaved by Helen Keller, (Leslie Fulenwider, 1929)

White Teeth by Zadie Smith (Vintage, 2001)

With Love by Jane Goodall (North-South Books, 1998)

The Writing Life by Annie Dillard (Harper Perennial, 2013)

Wouldn't Take Nothing for My Journey Now by Maya Angelou (Bantam, 1994)

ABOUT THE AUTHOR

MEERA LEE PATEL is a self-taught artist and writer who believes that anything is possible.

She is the author of *My Friend Fear: Finding Magic in the Unknown*, a beautiful meditation on fear and how it can help us become who we really are—if we let it.

She is also the author of the bestselling *Start Where You Are: A Journal for Self-Exploration* and *Made Out of Stars: A Journal for Self-Realization*.

She lives with her husband, dog, innumerable black vultures, wild turkeys, coyotes, and prancing deer on a farm in the northern woods of Nashville, Tennessee.

For more information, please visit meeralee.com or find her online @meeraleepatel.